THE WAR POWERS RESOLUTION

THE WAR POWERS RESOLUTION
THE ROLE OF CONGRESS IN U.S. ARMED INTERVENTION

PAT M. HOLT

American Enterprise Institute for Public Policy Research
Washington, D.C.

Pat M. Holt was chief of staff of the Senate Foreign Relations Committee from 1974 to 1977 after having served as a member of the committee's professional staff since 1950.

ISBN 0-8447-3299-0

Library of Congress Catalog Card No. 78-9571

AEI Studies 197

© 1978 by American Enterprise Institute for Public Policy Research, Washington, D.C. Permission to quote from or to reproduce materials in this publication is granted when due acknowledgment is made.

Printed in the United States of America

CONTENTS

1	INTRODUCTION	1
2	THE RESOLUTION AND ITS ANTECEDENTS	3
3	HAS THE PRESIDENT COMPLIED?	11
4	CAN THE RESOLUTION WORK?	23
5	EXECUTIVE-CONGRESSIONAL RELATIONS IN TIMES OF CRISIS	31
6	CONCLUSION	37
	APPENDIX: The War Powers Resolution	41

1
Introduction

The War Powers Resolution represented an attempt by Congress to do something which, as former Undersecretary of State George Ball put it,[1] the Founding Fathers thought they could not do—namely, to spell out the dividing line between the constitutional power of Congress to declare war and the constitutional power of the President as commander-in-chief. When the resolution (P.L. 93-148) became law on November 7, 1973, over President Nixon's veto, it was the culmination of three years of congressional consideration and at least twice as many years of mounting congressional frustration with the Indochinese policies of both the Johnson and the Nixon administrations.

The Nixon veto was based on grounds of unconstitutionality, a question which has spawned a voluminous and inconclusive scholarly literature and which will not be reexamined here. A short, nonlegal summary of the issue is that, at any given moment, the relative powers of the President and Congress are what either feels it can get away with. In any event, the problem addressed by the War Powers Resolution is at least as much political as it is constitutional and will most likely be settled, if at all, through political rather than judicial processes. Both supporters and opponents of the resolution in the Senate have expressed doubts that the Supreme Court will ever rule on the issue.

The fact that the resolution became law only over the President's veto destroyed one of the objectives of its principal sponsor in the Senate, Jacob Javits (R-N.Y.). It had been Javits's hope that Congress would work out a "methodology," as he called it, for joint presidential-congressional action in sending American troops into combat, that the

---

[1] U.S. Congress, Senate, *War Powers Legislation*, Hearings before the Committee on Foreign Relations, 92d Congress, 1st session (1972), p. 621.

President would sign it, and that the resulting law would then represent a compact between Congress and the President for making the Constitution work in what is generally admitted to be a gray area. But the veto meant that the President would not accept any part of it, and left the result somewhat cloudier than it would have been otherwise.

President Ford also challenged the constitutionality of the law, though he made reports required by it on four occasions. President Carter, on the other hand, has described the law as providing for an appropriate reduction of the powers that the President had before Vietnam.[2] Herbert J. Hansell, the legal adviser of the Carter State Department, has told the Senate Foreign Relations Committee that the Carter administration does not challenge the law under the Constitution, but, he added cautiously, this was not the same as saying it was constitutional. Indeed, he was not prepared to say that the administration would find it constitutional in all respects.[3]

With the idea of a compact perhaps still lurking in the back of his mind, Javits pressed Hansell to formalize agreed procedures under the resolution. He suggested a letter from the President to the speaker and the president pro tempore of the Senate.[4] Such a letter has not been forthcoming, though there have been inconclusive lower level discussions.

The problems raised by the War Powers Resolution go far beyond constitutional issues and raise questions about the practical operation of the government, such as:

- How can Congress participate in making the decisions required in times of crisis?
- Does Congress really want to participate?
- Would it be more in the national interest if Congress were to participate to a greater extent than has usually been the case?
- Does the War Powers Resolution provide an effective way for Congress to participate?

An examination of past experience with the War Powers Resolution provides only partial, inconclusive answers to these questions, but it does serve to illuminate the problem and to define the issues.

---

[2] In responding to a question during his telephone question-and-answer broadcast in March 1977.
[3] U.S. Congress, Senate, *War Powers Resolution*, Hearings before the Committee on Foreign Relations, 95th Congress (1977), p. 207.
[4] Ibid., p. 204.

2
The Resolution and Its Antecedents

The War Powers Resolution (for the complete text see the Appendix) is a short, but extraordinarily complicated, piece of legislation. In essence, it lays out the following procedure: *Before* American troops are introduced "into hostilities or into situations where imminent involvement in hostilities is clearly indicated by the circumstances," the President is to consult with Congress "in every possible instance." *After* troops are so introduced, in the absence of a declaration of war, the President is to submit a report to Congress within forty-eight hours. Then, sixty days—or in special circumstances ninety days—after that, the involvement of the troops is to be terminated, *unless* Congress has taken affirmative action in the meantime to approve it. Congress can also terminate the involvement before sixty days have elapsed by passing a concurrent resolution (which does not require the President's signature and is therefore not subject to a veto).

The legislative precursor of the War Powers Resolution was the National Commitments Resolution (S. Res. 85, 91st Cong., agreed to June 25, 1969, by a vote of 70–16). As a simple Senate resolution, it did not require the concurrence of the House.

The operative paragraph of the National Commitments Resolution reads in its entirety:

> That (1) a national commitment for the purpose of this resolution means the use of the Armed Forces of the United States on foreign territory, or a promise to assist a foreign country, government, or people by the use of the Armed Forces or financial resources of the United States, either immediately or upon the happening of certain events, and by the United States results only from affirmative action (2) it is the sense of the Senate that a national commitment

taken by the executive and legislative branches of the United States Government by means of a treaty, statute, or concurrent resolution of both Houses of Congress specifically providing for such commitment.

This resolution was the Senate's reaction to the repeated references, mainly by Secretary of State Dean Rusk, to the U.S. "commitment" in Vietnam. It was a way of telling the administration that the Senate recognized no such commitment. More important, it carried the message that, if there were to be a commitment, Congress (or at least the Senate, through a treaty) would have to participate in the decision. The Foreign Relations Committee described the resolution as "an invitation to the executive to reconsider its excesses, and to the legislature to reconsider its omissions, in the making of foreign policy."[5]

If nothing more had happened in Southeast Asia, probably no further action would have been taken. The Foreign Relations Committee said as much in its 1972 report on the first war powers bill to reach the Senate calendar: "Following upon adoption of the National Commitments Resolution it was hoped that the then newly installed Nixon Administration would take a view different from that of its predecessor. That hope has not been realized."[6]

The U.S. incursion into Cambodia in May 1970 triggered a flurry of bills on war powers in both the House and the Senate. The first Senate bill (S. 3964, 91st Cong.) was introduced on June 15, 1970, by Senator Javits with the cosponsorship of Senator Bob Dole (R-Kan.), who was to become President Ford's running mate in the 1976 election.

On November 16, the House, by a vote of 288–39, passed a joint resolution (H.J. Res. 1355, 91 Cong.) which asked the President to consult with Congress "whenever feasible" before involving troops in hostilities. The resolution required reports of such actions after the fact. No action was taken in the Senate. The following year the House, by voice vote, passed a similar joint resolution (H.J. Res. 1, 92d Cong.), deleting the qualifying phrase "whenever feasible."

Meanwhile, the Senate Foreign Relations Committee had been holding extensive but intermittent hearings, and in December Javits introduced a revised bill. He was joined by a number of other senators including, significantly, John Stennis (D-Miss.), chairman of the Armed Services Committee. This bill (S. 2956, 92d Cong.) was re-

---

[5] S. Rept. 91-129 (91st Cong., 1st sess.), p. 30.
[6] S. Rept. 92-206 (92d Cong., 2d sess.), p. 8.

ported by the Foreign Relations Committee on February 9, 1972, with only minor amendments. It passed the Senate on April 13 by a vote of 68–16, with Senator Dole, the cosponsor of the original Javits bill, voting nay. By a vote of 22–56 the Senate rejected a substitute, similar to H.J. Res. 1, offered by Senator Peter Dominick (R-Colo.).

S. 2956 was much more far-reaching than H.J. Res. 1 and much closer to what eventually became the law. It spelled out three situations in which the President could involve the armed forces in hostilities without specific authorization by Congress: (1) an attack on the United States, (2) an attack on U.S. armed forces stationed abroad, and (3) the evacuation of American citizens abroad under "a direct and imminent threat to their lives." But such involvement of U.S. troops could continue for no more than thirty days without specific authorization by Congress, and Congress could terminate it, before thirty days had elapsed, by an act or joint resolution.

Because of the great differences between the House joint resolution and the Senate bill, and the attendant controversy, a good deal of parliamentary maneuvering ensued. In the course of this, the House again (on August 1) passed the text of H.J. Res. 1, this time as a substitute for S. 2956, by a vote of 344–13. Conferees were finally appointed, but they met only once, near the end of the Congress, and did not reach agreement.

In 1973 the committees in both House and Senate again started afresh. The Senate Foreign Relations Committee reported its bill (S. 440, 93d Cong.) on June 14; the House Foreign Affairs Committee reported its bill (H.J. Res. 542, 93d Cong.) on June 15. S. 440 was identical to S. 2956, which the Senate had passed the year before.

The major change was in the House bill. Although the House had previously lagged behind the Senate in asserting congressional powers, it now shot ahead. The House bill not only provided for the withdrawal of American forces from hostilities within 120 days unless Congress approved their involvement; it also provided for the termination of certain peaceful foreign deployments, that is, the commitment abroad of forces equipped for combat "except for deployments which relate solely to supply, replacement, repair or training" and substantial enlargements of combat-equipped forces already deployed abroad. Furthermore, forces could be ordered to withdraw from both hostilities and foreign deployments by a concurrent resolution. The House bill also applied, as the Senate bill did not, to current hostilities, that is, to those in Southeast Asia.

The technical distinction between a bill or joint resolution, on the one hand, and a concurrent resolution on the other, is crucial.

For practical purposes, there is no difference between a bill and a joint resolution. Both must pass both houses of Congress and are then sent to the President; if he signs them, or if they are passed over his veto, they become laws. A concurrent resolution must be passed by both houses of Congress, but it does not go to the President, and it does not have the force of law. The provision of the War Powers Resolution for the withdrawal of troops upon passage of a concurrent resolution is a procedure designed to avoid a possible presidential veto. This procedure has been used by Congress for years, with increasing frequency, for a wide range of both domestic and foreign activities. Every President since Franklin Roosevelt has argued that it is unconstitutional.

The House passed its war powers bill, with amendments, on July 18, 1973, by a vote of 244–170. The most important amendment deleted the application of the bill to current hostilities. The Senate passed its bill, with minor amendments, on July 20 by a vote of 72–18. In working out the compromise which eventually became law, the conferees adopted the general approach of the House bill, with two important differences. They dropped the provision that gave Congress a concurrent resolution veto on major peaceful foreign deployments, though they retained the requirement that the President report to Congress on these deployments. And they abandoned the section of the Senate bill that spelled out the circumstances in which U.S. armed forces could be involved in hostilities. In its place, they provided that

> the constitutional powers of the President as Commander-in-Chief to introduce United States Armed Forces into hostilities, or into situations where imminent involvement in hostilities is clearly indicated by the circumstances, are exercised only pursuant to (1) a declaration of war, (2) specific statutory authorization, or (3) a national emergency created by attack upon the United States, its territories or possessions, or its armed forces. [Sec. 2(c)]

This statement omits the reference in the Senate bill to the President's authority to use the armed forces for the evacuation of American citizens. Furthermore, the kind of national emergency in which the armed forces may be used is limited to one created by attack on the United States or its armed forces, thereby omitting emergencies created by attacks on American civilians abroad.

The joint explanatory statement of the conference committee yields no clue as to what significance, if any, the conferees attached to these omissions. A widely held view, reinforced by many precedents, is that the President does have constitutional authority to protect and evacuate American citizens from dangerous situations abroad. But there is dispute as to how far this authority can be carried before it begins to take on some aspects of extraterritoriality and becomes inconsistent with the principle that when American citizens go abroad they leave behind the protection of the United States.

The conferees apparently intended this section of the law to be simply a statement of the status quo. If this is so, and if they did indeed take for granted the President's authority to evacuate Americans, their failure to mention it is all the more puzzling, especially since the Senate bill made specific provision for such circumstances. It limited the President's power of unilateral action to the protection of American citizens, while evacuating them

> as rapidly as possible, from (A) any situation on the high seas involving a direct and imminent threat to the lives of such citizens and nationals, or (B) any country in which such citizens and nations are present with the express or tacit consent of the government of such country and are being subjected to a direct and imminent threat to their lives, either sponsored by such government or beyond the power of such government to control.

In the latter case, the President was to make "every effort" to end the threat without using the armed forces and was also, where possible, to obtain the consent of the foreign government concerned.[7]

The Senate agreed to the conference report on October 10 by a vote of 75–20, and the House agreed on October 12 by a vote of 238–123. President Nixon vetoed the resolution on October 24, 1973. "The restrictions which this resolution would impose upon the authority of the President," he said, "are both unconstitutional and dangerous to the best interests of our Nation." He argued that the resolution "would have vastly complicated or even made impossible" the American response to the Berlin crisis of 1961, the Cuban missile crisis of 1962, the Congo rescue operation of 1964, and the Jordanian crisis of 1970. It would, he said,

> undercut the ability of the United States to act as an effective influence for peace. For example, the provision automatically

---

[7] It should be noted that early drafts of war powers legislation included protection of American property, as well as of American citizens, among the purposes for which the President could unilaterally use the armed forces abroad. This idea was dropped at an early stage by general agreement.

cutting off certain authorities after 60 days unless they are extended by the Congress could work to prolong or intensify a crisis. Until the Congress suspended the deadline, there would be at least a chance of United States withdrawal and an adversary would be tempted therefore to postpone serious negotiations until the 60 days were up. Only after the Congress acted would there be a strong incentive for an adversary to negotiate. In addition, the very existence of a deadline could lead to an escalation of hostilities in order to achieve certain objectives before the 60 days expired.

The resolution, he argued, would also "strike from the President's hand a wide range of important peacekeeping tools by eliminating his ability to exercise quiet diplomacy backed by subtle shifts in our military deployments." Finally, "it would give every future Congress the ability to handcuff every future President merely by doing nothing and sitting still."[8]

The President's arguments were to no avail. The House voted to override his veto 284–135 on November 7, and the Senate followed suit a few hours later, 75–18. There had never been any doubt about the outcome in the Senate. In four votes on roughly similar measures over a nineteen-month period, the majority in the Senate was consistently four to one—68–16 in April 1972; 72–18 in June 1973; 75–20 in October 1973; and 75–18 in November 1973.

In the House, however, matters were different. Its 244–170 vote to pass the resolution was 32 votes short of the two-thirds majority needed to override a veto; its vote of 238–123 on the conference report was 3 votes short. But the House did override the veto by four votes more than needed. Despite fluctuations in the total number of members voting, there was a steady accretion of support for the resolution. Or perhaps the trend should be described as a steady erosion of support for the President, the result of the growing unpopularity of the war in Vietnam compounded by the unfolding Watergate scandal.

The vote on overriding came less than three weeks after the "Saturday Night Massacre" when Attorney General Elliot Richardson and Deputy Attorney General William Ruckelshaus resigned rather than carry out the President's order to fire Watergate Special Prosecutor Archibald Cox. The Nixon political fortunes were at their lowest point to that time. The vote also came shortly after the Yom Kippur War in the Middle East, during which U.S. armed forces had

---

[8] H. Doc. 93-171 (93d Cong., 1st sess.).

been put on alert in the middle of the night, and U.S. Air Force cargo planes had resupplied Israel. This crisis alarmed some people in Congress, but it would not have led the large and influential pro-Israeli bloc in the House to put restrictions on the President's authority.

Sentiment in the House was clearly changing before either the Yom Kippur War or the Saturday Night Massacre. The resolution which the House passed by 244–170 in July 1973 was a far cry from the pallid resolutions it had passed in 1970 and 1971—resolutions which the Nixon administration had said it would accept. The distance the House had moved from 1970 to 1973 is a measure, more than anything else, of the growing unpopularity of the war in Vietnam. As a consequence of two elections during this period, there were 117 members of the House in 1973 who had not been members in 1970. During this same period, Congress also became steadily more assertive in using its power of the purse to force a liquidation of the war, and in the summer of 1973 it prohibited the use of any funds for military activities in Indochina. Still, the House overrode the veto by a margin of only 4 votes out of 419 cast. One can only speculate about whether those four votes would have stayed with the President in the absence of the Saturday Night Massacre, or whether the surge of antiwar sentiment would have been sufficient.

3
Has the President Complied?

It is indicative of the controversy surrounding the War Powers Resolution that there is not even agreement about how many times it has come into play, or indeed whether it has even been complied with while its procedures were being followed. President Ford sent Congress the reports required by the resolution on four occasions, all within a period of six weeks, in April and May 1975. These reports were in connection with evacuations from Danang, Phnom Penh, and Saigon in April, and the rescue of the S.S. *Mayaguez* and its crew from Cambodia in May.

In a speech at the University of Kentucky in April 1977, Ford said that he had also followed the resolution's procedures in the case of two evacuation operations in Lebanon in 1976,[9] but no written reports from the President, either pursuant to the resolution or otherwise, were ever received by Congress. According to officials of the State Department, certain information was provided informally to selected members of the congressional leadership, but this kind of procedure has been routine for years and certainly does not qualify as complying with, or even "taking note of" (Ford's words), the War Powers Resolution. Ford also said in Kentucky that he did not think that the resolution applied even in the case of Vietnam and Cambodia, nor did he concede that it was constitutionally binding on the President.

Senator Eagleton thought that the resolution also applied to the use of twenty-two helicopters sent to rescue Americans from Cyprus during the disorders on the island in July 1974, and called the lack

---

[9] Gerald R. Ford, press release, April 11, 1977, p. 2.

of a report a "glaring and serious omission of law";[10] but the issue was not pressed.

The circumstances of the four operations in Southeast Asia about which President Ford submitted War Powers Resolution reports to Congress and of the Lebanon operation, about which he did not submit a report, follow.[11]

Danang. In late March and early April 1975, as the position of the South Vietnamese government began to collapse throughout the country, massive numbers of refugees began fleeing areas northwest of Danang that were overrun or threatened by the Viet Cong and North Vietnamese. They represented a serious problem of public safety, even in the areas still controlled by the Saigon government, as well as a threat to the evacuation of the remaining Americans.

In these circumstances, efforts were begun to move the refugees by sea to points farther south. Congress was in its Easter recess at the time, but members of the leadership were informed late on Saturday afternoon, March 30, of U.S. participation in the refugee evacuation. It was apparently originally contemplated (or hoped) that this could be undertaken by merchant vessels under charter. As the situation deteriorated, however, President Ford ordered the participation of a navy amphibious task force, including twelve helicopters and 700 marines. The first naval vessel entered South Vietnamese waters on April 3, and the last departed on April 11. In all, 65,000 refugees were transported from the vicinity of Danang.

The President submitted his report on April 4, "taking note"—as he put it—of Sec. 4(a)(2) of the War Powers Resolution, the provision that applies to the introduction of combat-equipped forces into a nonhostile environment. The law's requirement for consultation does not apply to actions taken under this provision. The main purpose of the Marines was to maintain order among the refugees aboard ship. Although Ford did not say so, the navy task force was under orders to avoid combat.

Phnom Penh. On the same day that the Danang sealift was completed, the collapse of the Lon Nol government in Cambodia made it necessary to evacuate the remaining Americans in Phnom Penh. The forces

---

[10] *Congressional Record*, July 31, 1974, p. 25916.

[11] The texts of all four reports may be found in U.S. Congress, House of Representatives, *The War Powers Resolution: Relevant Documents, Correspondence, Reports*, Subcommittee on International Security and Scientific Affairs of the Committee on International Relations, 94th Congress, 2d session (January 1976).

involved were thirty-six helicopters, 350 marines, fighter air cover, and command and control elements. The purpose of the marines was to protect the helicopter landing zone near the American embassy in Phnom Penh. The first helicopter landed at 10:00 P.M. EDT on April 11; the last helicopter departed two hours and twenty minutes later and was fired at from the ground but was not hit. In all, 82 Americans, 159 Cambodians, and 35 nationals of other countries were evacuated.

The President reported to Congress on April 12, "taking note" of Section 4 of the War Powers Resolution but without specifying a subsection. He noted that the U.S. forces were "equipped for combat within the meaning of Section 4(a)(2)." Although the law does not require consultation in such cases, congressional leaders were informed of developments, a procedure that Monroe Leigh, legal adviser of the State Department, later equated with "consultation."[12] Most members of Congress generally found the Phnom Penh operation a model of smooth efficiency, especially in contrast to the storm which was about to break over Saigon.

Saigon. The situation in Saigon was complicated by the related, but different, problems of, on the one hand, evacuating Americans and, on the other, of evacuating Vietnamese or otherwise helping those who wanted to leave to do so. The administration understandably felt an obligation to many thousands of Vietnamese, ranging all the way from those who had been directly employed by the Americans to those who had otherwise identified themselves with the United States. It wished to preserve, for as long as possible, as many options as possible for these Vietnamese to leave the country.

Until shortly before the end, many Vietnamese and some Americans were flying out of Saigon using regular commercial air service as well as commercial charters and air force transports. It was a fine question as to how long these means could be used before Saigon fell to the Viet Cong and North Vietnamese or public order collapsed. Either of these events would have made the evacuation of Americans possible, if at all, only through the use of military force. In addition, a mass exodus of Americans would have created panic. Indeed, Americans found it prudent to conceal from their Vietnamese servants evidence of packing or other preparations for departure.

---

[12] U.S. Congress, House of Representatives, *War Powers: A Test of Compliance Relative to the Danang Sealift, the Evacuation of Phnom Penh, the Evacuation of Saigon, and the Mayaguez Incident*, Hearings before the Subcommittee on International Security and Scientific Affairs of the Committee on International Relations, 94th Congress, 1st session (1975), p. 5.

Against this background, there was a deep-seated congressional distrust, especially among members of the Senate Foreign Relations Committee, of Graham Martin, the U.S. Ambassador to South Vietnam. This distrust fed a suspicion that Martin, and perhaps Ford and Kissinger as well, would delay the evacuation of Americans in favor of the evacuation of Vietnamese. This suspicion was also nourished by skepticism in the Senate about the administration's frequent predictions of a "bloodbath" which would follow a North Vietnamese/Viet Cong victory. While sympathetic to the plight of pro-American Vietnamese, many senators did not share the fervor this plight aroused in some administration spokesmen.

All of these things contributed to a fear in Congress that the evacuation of Americans would be delayed until a major military operation was required, and that such an operation would be expanded to include the evacuation of Vietnamese. These anxieties were reinforced by the confidential report of two staff members sent to Saigon in April 1975 by the Foreign Relations Committee, which did not fully trust the information it was receiving from the State Department.

Congress also found incredible the administration's justification for continued aid to Vietnam, even the amount included in the budget submitted to Congress earlier in 1975. While admitting the perilous situation of the Saigon government, the administration argued that, with continued American aid, South Vietnam had a chance for survival. Members of Congress noted, but discounted, the difficulties of the administration's situation. Although it might have privately agreed that the Saigon government was doomed, a public indication that it thought so would certainly have sealed South Vietnam's fate, and, furthermore, would have subjected the administration to the charge of "selling out" its former ally.

As late as April 10 President Ford asked Congress for almost $1 billion in additional aid for South Vietnam. At the same time, in order to provide for evacuation, he asked for clarification of seven provisions of law that prohibited the use of appropriations for military operations in Southeast Asia.

Monroe Leigh set forth the administration's view before the House International Relations Committee (the name had been changed from Foreign Affairs in January) on April 16. He held that limitations on the use of funds, and not the War Powers Resolution, prevented the use of U.S. armed forces to evacuate Vietnamese nationals. The President, Leigh said, did not need additional authority to evacuate Americans. Nor would he need additional authority to evacuate the Vietnamese if they were in a nonhostile environment. But he could not use funds to evacuate Vietnamese from an area of hostilities without violating the law. The members of the committee did not seem wholly persuaded.

Meanwhile, as hostilities drew closer to Saigon every day, Congress was even more anxious than the President to evacuate Americans. The Senate Foreign Relations Committee went to the White House in a body on April 14 to urge the President to do so posthaste. This was the first meeting of the committee with a President since it met with President Woodrow Wilson about the Versailles Treaty.

Both the Senate (on April 23) and the House (on April 24) voted to give the President some of the authority and a little of the money that he had requested. The Senate and House bills differed in detail but not in their basic thrust, which was to hedge the President's authority so as to ensure that the evacuation of any Vietnamese was incidental to the evacuation of Americans, and not the principal purpose of the operation. Both bills had provisions relating the matter to the War Powers Resolution. As these provisions emerged from conference, they specifically authorized the introduction of U.S. troops into hostilities, pursuant to the War Powers Resolution. Also invoked were those sections of the resolution that limited the troops' presence to sixty days, unless extended by Congress, and that provided for withdrawal of the troops by concurrent resolution at any time.

The conference report was agreed to by the Senate, 46–17, on April 25, but consideration in the House was delayed until May 1. By that time the Saigon government had collapsed, the bill was overtaken by events, and the House rejected the conference report by a vote of 162–246.

President Ford had ordered American forces to proceed with the evacuation on April 28. During a period of twenty hours on April 29 (April 29–30 Saigon time), a force of seventy helicopters and 865 marines took out 1,373 Americans, 5,595 Vietnamese, and 85 nationals of other countries from landing zones near the American embassy and the Defense Attaché Office at Ton Son Nhut Airfield. A few Americans were also evacuated by sea from Can Tho. There was some fighting during the course of the operation, but the only American casualties were two crew members of a navy helicopter lost at sea. President Ford reported this to Congress, "taking note" of Section 4 of the War Powers Resolution, on April 30.

Although fighting was minimal and casualties were light, the evacuation clearly took place in a hostile environment and therefore put the President at least technically in violation of the numerous limitations on using funds for military activities in Vietnam. The evacuation of the Vietnamese was a violation, even by Monroe Leigh's interpretation of April 16. On May 7, however, Leigh offered a clarification. The President, he said, "wanted the political support of the Congress in what he saw was going to be necessary, and the fact that he asked for it should not, in my view, be interpreted as an indication of his belief that in the absence of congressional action he could not have done the things that he did."[13]

Nevertheless, the evacuation could be counted an operational success, and there was little disposition in Congress to quibble. The resolution's requirement for consultation had been met (albeit more at the initiative of Congress than of the President), and the burden of the advice the President had received from Congress was to undertake the evacuation sooner rather than later. Although Congress was content to leave well enough alone, comments by members of the House International Relations Committee made it clear that the issue of the President's authority was still far from settled.[14]

Mayaguez. Much greater controversy attended the rescue of the *Mayaguez*. This U.S. merchant ship, with an American crew of thirty-nine, was seized by Cambodian patrol boats in international waters off the coast of Cambodia while en route from Hong Kong to Thailand on May 12, 1975.

The first involvement of U.S. armed forces came within a few hours when a reconnaissance plane was dispatched from Utapao, Thailand, to locate the ship. During the course of the day, the aircraft carrier *Coral Sea* and other ships of the Seventh Fleet were ordered to the Gulf of Siam, the 3rd Marine Division on Okinawa was put on combat alert, and 1,100 marines were ordered flown from Okinawa and the Philippines to Utapao.

On the evening of May 12 (Washington time—morning of May 13 Cambodian time), a U.S. reconnaissance aircraft located the ship, which was being escorted by Cambodian gunboats. The aircraft was fired at and hit, sustaining minor damage. Later that day, the *Mayaguez* was observed at anchor near Koh Tang Island as its crew was being transferred from the ship. The President took steps in the early morning of May 13 (Washington time) to prevent the ship and crew from being taken to the Cambodian mainland, where their recovery would become more difficult. He ordered that Koh Tang Island be isolated, that movement be prevented between the ship and

---

[13] Ibid., p. 18.
[14] Ibid.

the island or the mainland, and that movement of the ship itself be prevented. In the course of carrying out these orders, U.S. aircraft sank three Cambodian patrol boats and damaged four others. These efforts were unsuccessful, however, in preventing the transfer of the crew to the mainland port of Kompong Som.

Meanwhile, diplomatic efforts to secure the release of the ship and crew were unsuccessful. These efforts proceeded first through the People's Republic of China and then through the secretary general of the United Nations. Premier Kukrit Pramoj of Thailand announced, as early as midday May 13 that he would not permit the use of Thai air bases for American military operations against Cambodia. Twenty-four hours later he made a formal protest and demanded that American marines be removed from Thailand by the next morning.

In the late afternoon of May 14 President Ford ordered an assault on Koh Tang Island, the boarding of the *Mayaguez*, and attacks against airfields and other military targets on the mainland in the vicinity of Kompong Som. In the course of these operations the crew of the *Mayaguez* turned up in a Thai fishing boat and were taken aboard the U.S. destroyer *Wilson*.

The marines attacking Koh Tang ran into heavy fire. The *Mayaguez* boarding party found the ship empty. The naval aircraft from the *Coral Sea* that attacked the mainland destroyed approximately seventeen Cambodian aircraft and an undetermined number of amphibious craft. In all, the U.S. armed forces suffered forty-one fatalities in the process of rescuing thirty-nine crewmen.

"Taking note" of Section 4(a)(1) of the War Powers Resolution, the President reported to Congress in the early morning of May 15 (signing the letters to the speaker and president pro tem at 2:30 A.M. in order to meet the forty-eight hour deadline). The report confined itself to the operations directly related to the *Mayaguez* and did not mention the troop movements to Thailand.

There was a good deal more public furor over the *Mayaguez* incident than over the three previous cases involving the War Powers Resolution, though no one complained about the rescue of the ship and its crew. Indeed, after receiving a briefing from a deputy assistant secretary of state in closed session on the afternoon of May 14, the Senate Foreign Relations Committee issued a hastily written statement supporting the President "in the exercise of his Constitutional powers within the framework of the War Powers Resolution to secure the release of the ship and its men."

The controversy came, rather, from two other aspects of the incident. One argument concerned the policy that was followed and did not apply to the legality of the procedure under either the War Powers Resolution or the Constitution. It was charged that the United States had overreacted, that a hasty operation had resulted in too many American casualties, that the attacks on the Cambodian mainland were uncalled for, that the attack on Koh Tang Island was unnecessary because no Americans were there, and that, as evidenced by their own broadcasts before the attack began, the Cambodians intended to return the ship anyway (the broadcast made no mention of the crew).[15]

The other controversy was the charge, vigorously denied by administration spokesmen, that there had been a failure of consultation with Congress, as required by the War Powers Resolution.[16] This, as we shall see below, is a classic illustration of both the practical and the semantic difficulties in executive-congressional relations during a rapidly developing crisis.

News of the seizure of the *Mayaguez* arrived at the National Military Command Center in Washington at 5:12 A.M. May 12. The President was informed at 7:40 A.M. At noon the National Security Council held an emergency forty-five-minute meeting on the subject. The following morning, May 13, a second National Security Council meeting was held. At 5:30 that afternoon—thirty-six hours after the first report had reached Washington (though the news had, of course, been widely reported in the press in the meantime)—White House aides made their first contacts, according to State Department records, with members of Congress. They told ten representatives and eleven senators of the plan to use some kind of force.

The following morning, between 11:15 and noon on May 14, the same twenty-one members, plus one additional representative, were given what amounted to a factual report of the situation. That afternoon, the House International Relations Committee, the Senate Foreign Relations Committee, and the House Armed Services Committee were briefed by State and Defense Department officials. Finally, at 6:30 that evening, the President himself briefed seventeen congressional leaders on the orders that he had issued, an hour and a half earlier, for military operations.

In his formal report to Congress the President wrote, "In view of this illegal and dangerous act, I ordered, *as you have been previously advised*, United States military forces to conduct the necessary

---

[15] See, for example, Richard H. Rovere, "Letter from Washington," *The New Yorker*, May 26, 1975.
[16] See, for example, *War Powers: A Test of Compliance*, pp. 77–88.

reconnaissance" (emphasis supplied). Neither the Foreign Relations Committee nor the office of the president pro tem had any record of having been "previously advised." Indeed, Senator Eastland himself told the chief of staff of the committee that he had not been previously advised. When queried about this, a White House congressional relations officer said that Senator Eastland and the speaker had been previously advised orally on three separate occasions.

What emerges from this is that the White House was trying to keep key members of Congress informed of what was happening. During this process, Leigh later argued to the House International Relations Committee, "the congressional leadership did have an opportunity to express its views."[17] But the controlling fact is that members of Congress did not feel that they had been consulted.

Lebanon. In the spring of 1976, as the Lebanese civil war intensified, an amphibious task force was stationed near the Lebanese coast in case it had to evacuate the 1,400 Americans in the country.

On June 16 U.S. Ambassador Francis E. Meloy and Counselor of Embassy Robert O. Waring were ambushed and killed, along with the ambassador's Lebanese chauffeur. On the following day, Secretary of State Kissinger appeared before the House International Relations Committee. Although the agenda was to be the secretary's visits to Latin America, Western Europe, and Africa, the matter of Lebanon naturally came up. Kissinger told the committee that he expected decisions about evacuation of Americans to be made "within the next thirty-six hours."

Representative Clement J. Zablocki (D-Wis.), the principal sponsor of the War Powers Resolution in the House, pointed out that this would presumably involve U.S. armed forces and "would implement the provisions of the War Powers Resolution." He then asked, "Has there been any consultation with Congress on this issue?" The following exchange then took place:

> SECRETARY KISSINGER. There are several methods of evacuation being considered, not all of which involve the possible use of American military personnel. . . . If American military personnel are used, it will be a very short operation. In that case, of course, there would be consultation with the Congress to inform the Congress of the nature of the operation.
> MR. ZABLOCKI. Consultation or informing?
> SECRETARY KISSINGER. Well, it would be both. But realistically,

---
[17] Ibid.

the time period for consultation would have to be very short, because one would not want too much opportunity for opposition to develop.[18]

No one asked if Kissinger meant opposition in Congress or in Lebanon.

On June 18 the American embassy in Beirut strongly urged all Americans to leave, and on June 20 a landing craft picked up 110 Americans and 166 persons of twenty-five other nationalities from a Beirut beach. They had been escorted to the beach by members of Al Fatah, the Palestinian guerrilla group, and were transferred to the amphibious ship *Spiegel Grove*, which deposited them in Athens two days later. The U.S. military personnel who went onto the beach were unarmed, a fact that arguably put the operation beyond the scope of the War Powers Resolution.

About a month later, on July 16, the U.S. embassy in Beirut announced a further evacuation because of "the steady deterioration in living conditions and the uncertain security situation." This evacuation was to be carried out July 20 in a bus-car convoy from Beirut to Damascus, under the protection of Palestinians and the Syrian Army, but on July 19 the embassy announced postponement because of "advice we received that conditions would not be totally secure." Finally, on July 27, the navy again carried out the evacuation, this time taking out 160 Americans and 148 other foreigners.

Compliance in the Six Crises. All of these instances were short-lived, the longest lasting eight days, the shortest less than three hours. In this they were similar to numerous instances over the years in which Presidents have sent U.S. armed forces abroad without congressional authorization, in crisis situations. (By Henry Steele Commager's calculation, 95 percent of these interventions have lasted less than seven days.)[19] There was no significant controversy about the Danang sealift or the evacuations from Phnom Penh and Lebanon. The Saigon evacuation was controversial principally because critics felt that it was delayed too long, thereby incurring unnecessary risks.

The most controversial incident was that of the *Mayaguez*, on grounds of overreaction and lack of consultation. But congressional complaints about lack of consultation were made after the fact and largely in response to administration assertions that there had been

---

[18] U.S. Congress, House of Representatives, *Report of Secretary of State Kissinger on His Visits to Latin America, Western Europe, and Africa*, Hearings before Committee on International Relations, 94th Congress, 2d session (1976), p. 13.
[19] *War Powers Legislation*, p. 8.

consultation. The charge of "no consultation" has substance, but the prevailing sentiment in Congress at the time was to recover the ship and rescue the crew. There was some concern over the Thai protests and some nervousness about a renewed involvement in Cambodia, but it may be questioned whether advice from Congress would have run strongly against what was done.

Commenting after House hearings on the four incidents in Southeast Asia, Representative Zablocki concluded that the resolution had worked "reasonably well." He also found it "reasonable to assume that the potential for precipitous military action evidenced in the past has been mitigated." This assumption is indeed reasonable, but it may overstate the role of the War Powers Resolution and neglect the changed political climate as a factor in the mitigation. Zablocki went on to give the executive branch "only mixed marks on the adequacy of its compliance effort." It passed, in his view, on reporting, but failed on consultation.

Senator Javits, on the other hand, did not think much of the reporting:

> I believe . . . the format and mode of delivery of the four initial reports . . . to be questionable in law and unsatisfactory. Each of the reports has been cast in the form of a personal letter from the President to the Speaker of the House and the President Pro Tempore of the Senate. They are brief to the point of being in minimal compliance with the content requirements set forth in the law . . . almost worthless from an information point of view. They do not suggest a readiness within the Executive Branch to provide the full and timely disclosure of relevant facts and judgments which the reporting provisions of the law were designed to elicit.[20]

Although this is perhaps an excessively harsh judgment, the method of reporting does reveal at least a potential problem. The President sent his reports to Speaker Carl Albert and President Pro Tem James Eastland personally and not to their congressional offices. The Danang report, for example, was sent to Albert in Peking and to Eastland in Doddsville, Mississippi. This was done on April 4, a Friday. Although duplicate copies were sent to their Washington offices, the reports were not received by the Senate Foreign Relations and House International Relations Committees until Monday, April 7. In the case of the Phnom Penh report, there was a delay of two days, and in the

---

[20] *War Powers: A Test of Compliance*, p. 69.

case of the Saigon report, a delay of one day. Only the *Mayaguez* report was received by the committees the same day that it was sent to the speaker and the president pro tem. Under the circumstances, none of this was serious, and the Danang and Phnom Penh reports were complicated by the intervention of weekends, but the congressional machinery clearly did not function with the expeditiousness that other circumstances might require.

Zablocki concluded that "the executive branch proclivity is toward evasive and selective interpretation of the War Powers Resolution."[21] This is also perhaps an overly harsh judgment, particularly in view of the fact that the Ford administration thought that the law was unconstitutional and did not admit that it had to comply at all.

The four instances of 1975 did not provide a real test of executive compliance with the resolution nor of congressional response. That test is yet to come, either during the Carter administration (which does not challenge the constitutionality of the law) or a future administration. What the four instances of 1975 did provide was illumination of some of the technical difficulties of the law, as well as some of the larger problems of congressional-executive relations in times of crisis.

---

[21] Ibid., p. vi.

4
Can the Resolution Work?

Use of Armed Forces in Hostilities. The first technical difficulty in the law is in Section 2(c), which defines the constitutional powers of the President as commander-in-chief as they relate to the introduction of "United States Armed Forces into hostilities, or into situations where imminent involvement in hostilities is clearly indicated by the circumstances." These powers, the resolution says, "are exercised only pursuant to (1) a declaration of war, (2) specific statutory authorization, or (3) a national emergency created by attack upon the United States, its territories or possessions, or its armed forces."

Since both a declaration of war and specific statutory authorization require an act of Congress, this means that the President can act on his own authority in the case of hostilities or of an imminent threat of hostilities only when there is a national emergency caused by an attack on U.S. territory or on U.S. armed forces. This does not include a national emergency arising from other causes; nor does it include attacks on civilian Americans.

Beyond this, the law gives no hint of what a "national emergency" is, no doubt on the reasonable theory that although it may be hard to define, anybody can recognize one when he sees it. But what is a national emergency to one President may be only an incident to another—or, more important, to Congress. Although it is hard to imagine an attack on the United States which would not create a national emergency, several attacks on U.S. armed forces have fallen short of doing so. The most recent example is the shooting down of a helicopter over North Korea in the summer of 1977. Earlier examples in Korea are the seizure of the *Pueblo* and the attack on U.S. soldiers engaged in cutting down a tree in the demilitarized zone.

A reasonable purpose of Section 2(c) would be to prevent a President from overreacting to a minor threat, but the language goes further. Although it does not inhibit the President from redeploying forces, as was done in East Asia following the seizure of the *Pueblo*, it does prevent him from putting forces into situations where there is a clear threat of hostilities. It therefore limits the range of responses available to the President without reference to Congress. This may or may not be what the drafters of the resolution intended, but it is what they said.

Indeed, under this provision, the evacuation of Saigon and the rescue of the *Mayaguez* were both illegal. Although both were emergencies for the individuals involved, neither could reasonably be called a *national* emergency, and neither arose from an attack on U.S. territory. U.S. forces were fired on in both cases, but it was after the forces were introduced, not before.

Section 2(c) was the result of a compromise in the process of putting together the different approaches of the House and Senate bills. The Senate bill cataloged the circumstances in which the armed forces "may" be introduced in hostilities without a declaration of war or specific statutory authorization. The House bill did not; it simply provided a procedure for congressional termination of the involvement. The conference committee charged with resolving this difference generally followed the House approach but included Section 2(c) as a concession to the Senate. The heading of Section 2 is "Purpose and Policy," and (c) was intended to be neither an enlargement nor a restriction of the President's powers but rather a statement of them—a codification of the status quo. But this is not how it came out.

The problem of trying to catalog the situations in which the President has constitutional power of his own, independent of Congress, was one of the most troublesome that the authors of the resolution faced, and it is one with which Congress has continued to wrestle. While he was legal adviser of the State Department, Monroe Leigh submitted to the House International Relations Committee a detailed list of situations in which the President has independent authority, but warned that he thought it was incomplete.[22] His successor, Herbert J. Hansell, resisted attempts by the Senate Foreign Relations Committee to compile a similar list. In declining, he put his finger on the political, as distinguished from the legal, essence of the matter:

---

[22] Ibid., pp. 90–91.

> There is nothing that guarantees that a comprehensive list worked out with a congenial administration would deal with the problem that I think you are concerned about: what happens if you don't have a congenial administration? No catalog is going to deal with that problem. That is a problem we must face.[23]

Senator Javits has argued that when Section 2(c) is read in conjunction with Section 8, it is a reasonable but not exclusive list of powers.[24] Section 8 (see Appendix for text) deals at some length with interpretation of the resolution, but nowhere does it deal with the phrase in Section 2(c) that the powers of the President "are exercised *only* pursuant." [Emphasis added.] That is the flaw in the argument that Section 2(c) is not an *exclusive* list of powers.

Nevertheless, Senator Thomas Eagleton (D-Mo.), one of the original prime movers of war powers legislation, voted against the conference report on the grounds that it delegated congressional powers to the President. Eagleton's argument is based on the premise that Section 2(c) is nonbinding and nonenforceable and that, under the operative sections of the resolution, "the President has the unilateral authority to commit American troops anywhere in the world, under any conditions he decides, for 60 to 90 days."[25] The operative sections of the resolution do no more than Section 2(c) to provide sanctions or means of enforcement; they provide only a procedure which must be read against the background of Section 2(c).

Consultation. Section 2(c) and Section 3 of the resolution must also be taken together. Section 3 provides that

> the President in every possible instance shall consult with Congress before introducing United States Armed Forces into hostilities or into situations where imminent involvement in hostilities is clearly indicated by the circumstances, and after every such introduction shall consult regularly with the Congress until United States Armed Forces are no longer engaged in hostilities or have been removed from such situations.

The President cannot get a declaration of war or other specific statutory authorization without consulting Congress in any case. Therefore, all that Section 3 really adds, when read with Section 2(c), is a

---

[23] *War Powers Resolution*, p. 195.
[24] Ibid., p. 196.
[25] Ibid., p. 4.

requirement that the President consult "in every possible instance" before responding to a national emergency created by attack on the United States or its armed forces. Since during a real national emergency time is of the essence, there are not likely to be many instances in which consultation is possible. In any event, the law leaves that question, like the question of what is a national emergency, for later argument. The substantive problem involved here is how to make consultation work, not simply within the narrow requirements of the law but across the range of issues in foreign military policy. This problem will be discussed in a later section.

Presidential Reporting and Congressional Action. The law provides some complicated requirements for presidential reporting to Congress whenever certain troop movements are made "in the absence of a declaration of war." The first such case is whenever U.S. armed forces are introduced "into hostilities or into situations where imminent involvement in hostilities is clearly indicated by the circumstances" [Sec. 4(a)(1)]. The second case that requires presidential reporting involves the introduction of U.S. armed forces "into the territory, airspace or waters of a foreign nation, while equipped for combat, except for deployments which relate solely to supply, replacement, repair, or training of such forces" [Sec. 4(a)(2)]. The third case relates to the introduction "in numbers which substantially enlarge United States Armed Forces equipped for combat already located in a foreign nation" [Sec. 4(a)(3)]. It should be noted that there is no requirement for consultation with respect to the second and third cases, and a report is required only when troops are sent abroad, not when they are brought home.

The concern at the time was to give Congress more leverage over sending troops abroad, in part on the theory that although the Constitution may not permit the President to start a war, it gives him ample room to cause one. A body of opinion has now surfaced in Congress which puts a reverse twist on this and asserts that Congress has authority to keep troops overseas as well as to prevent them from being sent there in the first place. Thus Senator Sam Nunn (D-Ga.), arguing against the Carter plan for withdrawal from Korea, said, "If it [the War Powers Resolution] works one way, it works the other."[26] The resolution does not, of course, deal with this aspect, but both the House and Senate hearings are laced with suggestions by nongovernmental witnesses that Congress pay more attention to troop deploy-

---

[26] *Congressional Record*, June 16, 1977, p. S 9948 (daily edition).

ment in general and, specifically, play a role in determining how many troops should be sent where.

In any of the three cases spelled out in Section 4(a) the President must submit a written report within forty-eight hours to the speaker of the House and the president pro tempore of the Senate. With respect to the second and third cases—deployments—the report is the end of the matter. But the submission of a report in the case of hostilities begins another series of events. The involvement in hostilities cannot be continued longer than sixty days *unless* Congress "(1) has declared war or has enacted a specific authorization for such use of United States Armed Forces, (2) has extended by law such sixty-day period, or (3) is physically unable to meet as a result of an armed attack upon the United States" [Sec. 5(b)]. The President can secure an extension of the sixty-day period, for not more than thirty additional days, by certifying to Congress in writing that "unavoidable military necessity respecting the safety of United States Armed Forces requires the continued use of such armed forces in the course of bringing about a prompt removal of such forces" [Sec. 5(b)]. On the other hand, the sixty-day period can be shortened by a concurrent resolution [Sec. 5(c)]. (It is indicative of a significant body of congressional opinion, at least in 1973, that the House bill provided for a congressional veto of deployments, as well as of hostilities.)

Detailed provisions are made to expedite consideration of any bill or joint resolution which would remove or extend the sixty-day limitation, and there is also a schedule of deadlines for the several stages of congressional action (Sec. 6). A different set of procedures with its own set of deadlines is provided for congressional consideration of any concurrent resolution for the withdrawal of troops from hostile situations (Sec. 7). If all the time provided by these procedures were used, it would take forty-eight days to pass a concurrent resolution. This is only twelve days short of when the forces would have to be withdrawn anyway in the absence of congressional action—unless Congress had extended the sixty-day period and then thought better of it, or unless the President had extended it himself for up to thirty days by certifying "unavoidable military necessity."

Everything that follows the President's report is timed from the date he submits it. To guard against the possibility that a President would find some pretext not to submit a report, the law also dates the ensuing procedures from when the report "is required to be submitted." But it leaves open the question of who determines, and how, when the submission is required. A series of amendments submitted to the Foreign Relations Committee by Senator Eagleton in

July 1977 proposed that this determination be made by Congress in a concurrent resolution. But Eagleton made no provision for expediting the consideration of such a concurrent resolution, and one can imagine the sixty-day period or longer running while Congress wrangles over whether a report should have been submitted and, if so, when.

Eagleton also proposed an amendment requiring the President to specify the paragraph of Section 4(a) under which the report is submitted. Two of the four reports which Ford submitted were ambiguous in that they referred only to Section 4(a), thereby leaving in doubt whether they triggered the sixty-day period under Section 4(a)(1). In these cases, of course, the involvement was so brief that it did not matter, but one can imagine cases in which it would matter. One can also imagine cases in which an ingenious President could find a way to avoid the sixty-day period by specifying Section 4(a)(2) or 4(a)(3) instead of 4(a)(1).

There is also the question of what sort of troop movement is supposed to be reported under any of the three paragraphs of Section 4(a). One of Eagleton's amendments would include aerial bombardment in hostilities. But what about intermittent aerial bombardment, such as occurred at times in Vietnam? Does each episode constitute a new involvement, require a new report, and start a new sixty-day period? Even more puzzling, what about naval deployments? Sections 4(a)(2) and (3) speak of deployments in a "foreign nation," and therefore do not apply to movements of warships on the high seas. But what happens if an area of the high seas—for example, the Eastern Mediterranean—becomes an area of hostilities between third parties after the U.S. fleet is already there?

Interpretation. The resolution attempts in Section 8 to erect guideposts for interpretation, but only one of these is discussed here. This is the provision that authority to introduce the armed forces into hostilities or into hostile situations is not to be inferred

> from any treaty heretofore or hereafter ratified unless such treaty is implemented by legislation specifically authorizing the introduction of United States Armed Forces into hostilities or into such situations and stating that it is intended to constitute specific statutory authorization within the meaning of this joint resolution [Sec. 8(a)(2)].

This was the result of congressional frustration over the many arguments of the Johnson and Nixon administrations that the SEATO treaty underlay U.S. policy in Vietnam. But it raises a more serious question about NATO. In Article 5 of the North Atlantic Treaty the parties agree that "an armed attack against one or more of them in Europe or North America shall be considered an attack against them all." This means that the United States would view an attack against, say, Paris, as equivalent to an attack against, say, New York. Clearly, if an enemy struck New York the President would be expected to fight back instantaneously, as Roosevelt did after the attack on Pearl Harbor. There is a good deal in the legislative history of the North Atlantic Treaty to the effect that it is not, and was not intended to be, self-executing; but none of it seems to elude the clear meaning of Article 5.

This problem does not arise with respect to the several other security treaties to which the United States is a party. None of them is as specific or as far-reaching as the North Atlantic Treaty.

5
Executive-Congressional Relations in Times of Crisis

Presidential consultation with Congress, one of the major themes of the War Powers Resolution, has long been one of the major problems of executive-congressional relations, irrespective of the War Powers Resolution, and the resolution contributes little, if anything, toward its solution. In its report on the resolution (H. Rept. 93-287, 93d Cong.), the House International Relations Committee spelled out what it meant by "consultation":

> Rejected was the notion that consultation should be synonymous with merely being informed. Rather, consultation in this provision means that a decision is pending on a problem and that Members of Congress are being asked by the President for their advice and opinions and, in appropriate circumstances, their approval of action contemplated. Furthermore, for consultation to be meaningful, the President himself must participate and all information relevant to the situation must be made available.

This is reasonably close to what was done with respect to the Saigon evacuation, but it is quite different from the procedures followed in the other cases to which the War Powers Resolution has been applied, or in many other cases antedating the resolution. The executive branch has a long history of using "inform" synonymously with "consult." But even when it does not, a rare combination of circumstances is required to make the process work as described by the House committee. In the Saigon case, for example, Congress held strong views that it wanted to express directly to the President, and Congress was informed adequately on the progress of the evacuation, not only through its own staff but also through daily statistical reports, which it insisted on receiving prior to the involvement of American troops.

If Congress lacks both a strongly held view and sufficient information, there is unlikely to be meaningful consultation. Nowhere is this better illustrated than in the Cuban missile crisis of 1962, a situation which would have been covered by the War Powers Resolution if it had existed then. President Kennedy and a handful of his advisers considered the situation in utmost secrecy for a week. After deciding what to do, the President called in about twenty members of Congress to announce his decision to them two hours before he told the world. (Since Congress was adjourned at the time, he sent the air force throughout the country to fetch them.) This meeting, according to Theodore Sorensen's account, was "the only sour note of the day." The reason Sorensen found it so is revealing. The members of Congress, he says, reacted to the briefing "the same way most of us originally did." Later Kennedy remarked to Sorensen that "if they had gone through the five-day period we had gone through—in looking at the various alternatives, advantages and disadvantages . . . they would have come out the same way that we did."[27]

This is precisely the point. If Congress is to give informed advice, it must be informed, and it has to share the decision-making agonies of the executive branch. It is extremely doubtful that, if Kennedy had sent for even ten members of Congress when he first became aware of the missile crisis, any of them would have been willing to spend the next week as officials of the executive branch did—going through, as Kennedy put it, what "we had gone through." Even in fast-breaking crises, where less than a week is available for an initial decision, it is not sufficient for members of Congress to be briefed by the executive branch on the information available. It is crucial that they see the actual reports.

When President Johnson sent troops to the Dominican Republic in 1965 with the stated purpose of evacuating American citizens and nationals of other countries, there was initially little disposition in Congress to question the action. But as the intervention grew and the administration's justifications of it shifted, some senators expressed doubts. These led to an examination by the Foreign Relations Committee of the original cable traffic, and this in turn led some senators to take a view diametrically opposite that of the administration.

At the time of the Tonkin Gulf affair in 1964, nobody on Capitol Hill asked for the messages, though many later wished they had.

---

[27] Theodore C. Sorensen, *Kennedy* (New York: Harper & Row, 1965), p. 702.

When the cable traffic was later made available, it cast considerable doubt on the administration's original presentation of the facts. In the *Mayaguez* incident, despite questions about the administration's handling of the matter, both the Senate Foreign Relations Committee and the House International Relations Committee backed away from a real investigation, though the latter at least held a hearing.

Tonkin and *Mayaguez*, among many other examples which could be cited, illustrate one of the reasons why Congress is a sometime participant in crisis decision making. Senator Vandenberg said that Congress wanted to participate in the takeoffs as well as the crash landings; actually it sometimes seems more interested in investigating crash landings than in participating in takeoffs. Despite the fact that it was clumsily executed, *Mayaguez* was a success, and there is little political mileage to be gained in a post mortem of the rescue of American citizens and the protection of freedom of the seas. The Tonkin Gulf Resolution, on the other hand, was part of a chain of events leading to a highly unpopular war, and it became the subject of painstaking (and painful) reassessments.

After the failure of the Bay of Pigs invasion in 1961, the Senate Foreign Relations Committee held weeks of hearings rehashing all the bad advice Kennedy had received and trying to determine who had bungled what. After the success story of the missile crisis in 1962, Secretary of State Dean Rusk all but begged the Foreign Relations Committee to review—or investigate, if you will—the administration's handling of it, but no one was interested. The general principle seems to be that success has few autopsies; the corpse of a failure is picked to pieces.

The fact that Congress is interested in being consulted more at some times than at others (and is more available for consultation at some times than at others) has led to suggestions for a more institutionalized mechanism for consultation. It has been variously suggested that Congress ought to establish a super committee as a legislative counterpart of the National Security Council, or that specified members of Congress should be made statutory members of the NSC, or that there should be closer liaison at the staff level between the NSC and specified committees of Congress.[28] Another suggestion has been that, as part of the War Powers Resolution mech-

---

[28] See, for example, Francis O. Wilcox, *Congress, the Executive, and Foreign Policy* (New York: Harper & Row for the Council on Foreign Relations, 1971), pp. 157–59. See also, H.R. 7290 (92d Congress) by Representative Frank Horton; and testimony of George Reedy in *War Powers Legislation*, p. 456.

anism, Congress should establish a committee for consultation and require that a quorum of this committee always be in Washington.[29]

The approach of the Carter administration, in contrast to that of its predecessors, has been not to challenge the constitutionality of the legislation but rather to concentrate on the practical means for making it workable. To this end, it has been informally suggested that the leadership of each House should designate in advance a single person as the initial point of contact when a crisis develops. This individual would also be authorized to designate and activate perhaps eight to ten members of a small ad hoc committee which would meet as required.[30]

All of these suggestions are aimed at solving a problem that has been a source of frustration to the executive branch and of unhappiness to Congress—namely, who speaks for Congress? The answer, of course, is no one, and this is why the suggested arrangements have not been well received on Capitol Hill. The foreign affairs committees think they should be the primary point of contact; the leadership is jealous of its prerogatives; and the armed services committees do not want to be cut out.

A more profound problem of consultation is that—regardless whether it is thought that the President and Congress should be adversaries, or should be independent and deal with each other at arm's length, or should work together as a team—there is no way in which any group of members of Congress can participate in presidential decision making so as to add legal authority to the decision which results. Even if they concur in the decision, all they can add is political authority. If they do not concur, they can cause all manner of difficulties for the President. This is why it is simple political prudence for the President to involve them sooner rather than later, and to try to see to it that they do concur and lend political support. This is also why some members of Congress sometimes have resisted being drawn into executive branch decision making. They either feared that their participation would limit their future freedom of action, or they preferred not to share the political risks.

The President has to pick his way through a political minefield. It is clearly impractical for him to consult with 535 members of Congress. Considerations of time and security argue that the list of those chosen for consultation be short; so does the goal of having a

---

[29] Statement of Henry Steele Commager in *War Powers Legislation*, p. 17.

[30] Letter from Douglas J. Bennet, Jr., assistant secretary of state for congressional relations, to Senator John Sparkman, chairman, Foreign Relations Committee, August 2, 1977, in *War Powers Resolution*, pp. 199–203.

consensus emerge. But to the extent that the list is shortened, the risk increases of offending someone who is left out. And the risk also increases that those consulted may not reflect the majority opinion in the Congress. This explains a good deal of the furor in Congress over some of the misadventures of the Central Intelligence Agency. Selected members knew in advance and raised no objection, but they did not reflect the views of many of their colleagues.

The War Powers Resolution does not provide any method for consultation but leaves it up to the respective participants. This is probably best. Experience leads one to be skeptical of overly mechanistic procedures. Both members of Congress and Presidents are too individualistic and personalistic in their relations with each other for these procedures to work comfortably and well. Some of the best examples of executive-congressional consultation stem from the personal relationships which developed between President Truman and Senator Vandenberg, between Secretary Dulles and Senator George, and between President Kennedy and Senator Fulbright. Different methods have worked well or poorly at different times. But in the end, a President is going to make decisions in his own way, whatever the prescribed procedures to which he may pay lip service.

All of this begs the question whether the results, in terms of public policy, are better with or without adequate consultation. The question, indeed, has to be left hanging, because there is no basis in either history or political science for the view that superior wisdom resides in the executive branch or in Congress, though some of the argument over the War Powers Resolution has revolved around this point. Thus,

> SENATOR JAVITS. So really you are opposed to my bill because you have less faith in the Congress than you have in the President; isn't that true?
> SENATOR GOLDWATER. To be perfectly honest with you, you are right.[31]

---

[31] *War Powers Legislation*, p. 393.

6
Conclusion

Implicit in the War Powers Resolution and in much discussion of it is the view of Congress as a restraining influence on the President. But this view reflects the particular political environment in which the resolution was passed. In other times such as 1812 and 1898 the reverse was true.

What can be said for the War Powers Resolution is that by setting up a procedure—or what Javits has called a methodology—for precipitating a confrontation of the President and Congress, it has also provided an incentive, at both ends of Pennsylvania Avenue, to avoid one. At the same time, it increases the pressure on Congress by constructing a situation in which Congress either has to approve a military operation or take the responsibility for stopping it. The problem, as Senator Case put it, "is more a matter of making us [Congress] live up to our obligations than anything else."[32] In the more colorful phrase of Senator Javits, it gives Congress "the responsibility for putting the blood on our hands, too."[33] But the resolution is also constructed so that it gives the last word to Congress. To put it another way, it gives Congress a procedure for second-guessing the President.

Of course, Congress always has the last word anyway, and it has never been at a loss to find ways to second-guess the President when it wished to do so. Irrespective of presidential powers, Congress has a great many powers of its own, though it has frequently been reluctant to use them. Notable among these is the power of the purse.

Two of the amendments proposed to the War Powers Resolution

---

[32] *War Powers Resolution*, p. 179.
[33] Ibid., p. 182.

in the summer of 1977 would provide an automatic cutoff of appropriations in cases of unauthorized use of troops. In Senator Eagleton's version, the cutoff would apply whenever troops were used beyond the sixty-day period without specific authorization, and whenever they were used despite a concurrent resolution to the contrary. In the version of Representative Stephen Solarz (D-N.Y.), the cutoff would apply only after passage of a concurrent resolution.

Although some doubt has been expressed about the power of Congress to restrict appropriations after the fact,[34] there seems no doubt that Congress could, if it wished, make appropriations contingent in the first place. It also might well reexamine its own compliance with the constitutional provision that no military appropriation shall be for a period longer than two years. If this provision is being strictly observed, for example, how is it that the Pentagon estimates an unexpended balance of $80 billion, and an unobligated balance of $20 billion, at the end of the 1978 fiscal year?

The principal difficulty with the War Powers Resolution is likely to come from its effort to define with too much precision the authority of the President to act unilaterally. The result is to make that authority either too broad (in Eagleton's view) or too narrow (in Nixon's and Ford's). In retrospect, it would probably have been better to have followed the approach taken by the House in the drafting of the resolution—that is, to prescribe a procedure for congressional review of any use of U.S. troops abroad, whatever the reason or purpose.

Although the Senate Foreign Relations Committee held hearings in July 1977 to review the law, there seems to be little disposition, in either the Senate or the House, to reopen this particular Pandora's box, particularly in view of the Carter administration's preference to try to make it work rather than to tinker with it. Several senators who had voted for passage of the resolution now confess to second thoughts about it. Among these are the chairman and the ranking minority member of the Senate Foreign Relations Committee. The latter, Senator Clifford P. Case (R-N.J.), has said he probably would not have supported the resolution in the first place except for his respect and affection for Javits. Case described himself as a "benevolent skeptic" about the problems involved in the resolution.[35] Senator Frank Church (D-Idaho) summed it up:

> I voted for the bill because it came in the aftermath of the Vietnam experience and it seemed that Congress should at

---

[34] Testimony of Monroe Leigh, ibid., p. 76.
[35] Ibid., pp. 177–78.

> least endeavor to prevent another war initiated and pursued on the basis of executive decision.
>
> Still, I have had my doubts that it is possible to accomplish such an objective by statute . . . . [I]f the President . . . uses the Armed Forces in an action that is both swift and successful, then there is no reason to expect the Congress to do anything other than applaud.
>
> If the President employs forces in an action which is swift, but unsuccessful, then the Congress is faced with a fait accompli, and although it may rebuke the President, it can do little else.
>
> If the President undertakes to introduce American forces in a foreign war that is large and sustained, then it seems to me that the argument that the War Powers Resolution forces the Congress to confront that decision is an argument that overlooks the fact that Congress in any case must confront the decision, because it is the Congress that must appropriate the money to make it possible for the sustained action to be sustained.
>
> So, I wonder really whether we have done very much in furthering our purpose through the War Powers Resolution.[36]

The War Powers Resolution, in essence, is an effort by Congress to give itself more leverage in the tug of war with the executive branch. It would have raised fewer questions, but also provided less leverage, if it had been a concurrent resolution, or if it were now converted into one as Leigh and Goldwater have suggested.[37]

Nor should one lose sight of the fact that Congress felt it needed more leverage because of the growing feeling that two Presidents, one in each political party, had overstepped their authority in Vietnam. But, as these Presidents, especially Johnson, never tired of reminding their opponents in Congress (and infuriating them in the process), most of this had been done with at least the acquiescence of Congress (though not always, as in the case of the Tonkin Gulf Resolution, the informed acquiescence).

Thus, in the view of many of its supporters, the War Powers Resolution was nothing more than an attempt to restate and thereby reassert what they considered to be the ancient powers of Congress, powers which had atrophied through lack of use. At the same time, the authors of the resolution provided a procedure for the exercise of these powers in the future. It is a procedure, furthermore, which is

---

[36] Ibid., p. 172.
[37] Ibid., pp. 19, 77.

designed to force Congress to act, either to approve or to end any long-term U.S. military involvement abroad. If Congress does nothing, the involvement will end automatically after sixty or ninety days, and Congress will have the political responsibility for its own inaction. The War Powers Resolution, in short, is designed to make it more difficult for Congress to acquiesce in future situations like Vietnam. Whether it actually accomplishes that purpose depends less on the law itself than on whether Congress chooses to use the procedures and powers available to it.

APPENDIX
The War Powers Resolution

Public Law 93-148
93rd Congress, H. J. Res. 542
November 7, 1973

Joint Resolution

Concerning the war powers of Congress and the President.

Resolved by the Senate and House of Representatives of the United States of America in Congress assembled,   War Powers Resolution.

SHORT TITLE

SECTION 1. This joint resolution may be cited as the "War Powers Resolution".

PURPOSE AND POLICY

SEC. 2. (a) It is the purpose of this joint resolution to fulfill the intent of the framers of the Constitution of the United States and insure that the collective judgment of both the Congress and the President will apply to the introduction of United States Armed Forces into hostilities, or into situations where imminent involvement in hostilities is clearly indicated by the circumstances, and to the continued use of such forces in hostilities or in such situations.

(b) Under article I, section 8, of the Constitution, it is specifically provided that the Congress shall have the power to make all laws necessary and proper for carrying into execution, not only its own powers but also all other powers vested by the Constitution in the Government of the United States, or in any department or officer thereof.   USC prec. title 1.

(c) The constitutional powers of the President as Commander-in-Chief to introduce United States Armed Forces into hostilities, or into situations where imminent involvement in hostilities is clearly indicated by the circumstances, are exercised only pursuant to (1) a declaration of war, (2) specific statutory authorization, or (3) a national emergency created by attack upon the United States, its territories or possessions, or its armed forces.

CONSULTATION

SEC. 3. The President in every possible instance shall consult with Congress before introducing United States Armed Forces into hostilities or into situations where imminent involvement in hostilities is clearly indicated by the circumstances, and after every such introduction shall consult regularly with the Congress until United States Armed Forces are no longer engaged in hostilities or have been removed from such situations.

REPORTING

SEC. 4. (a) In the absence of a declaration of war, in any case in which United States Armed Forces are introduced—
  (1) into hostilities or into situations where imminent involvement in hostilities is clearly indicated by the circumstances;   87 STAT. 555
  (2) into the territory, airspace or waters of a foreign nation, while equipped for combat, except for deployments which relate solely to supply, replacement, repair, or training of such forces; or   87 STAT. 556
  (3) in numbers which substantially enlarge United States Armed Forces equipped for combat already located in a foreign nation;

Pub. Law 93-148   - 2 -   November 7, 1973

the President shall submit within 48 hours to the Speaker of the House of Representatives and to the President pro tempore of the Senate a report, in writing, setting forth—

    (A) the circumstances necessitating the introduction of United States Armed Forces;

    (B) the constitutional and legislative authority under which such introduction took place; and

    (C) the estimated scope and duration of the hostilities or involvement.

(b) The President shall provide such other information as the Congress may request in the fulfillment of its constitutional responsibilities with respect to committing the Nation to war and to the use of United States Armed Forces abroad.

(c) Whenever United States Armed Forces are introduced into hostilities or into any situation described in subsection (a) of this section, the President shall, so long as such armed forces continue to be engaged in such hostilities or situation, report to the Congress periodically on the status of such hostilities or situation as well as on the scope and duration of such hostilities or situation, but in no event shall he report to the Congress less often than once every six months.

CONGRESSIONAL ACTION

SEC. 5. (a) Each report submitted pursuant to section 4(a)(1) shall be transmitted to the Speaker of the House of Representatives and to the President pro tempore of the Senate on the same calendar day. Each report so transmitted shall be referred to the Committee on Foreign Affairs of the House of Representatives and to the Committee on Foreign Relations of the Senate for appropriate action. If, when the report is transmitted, the Congress has adjourned sine die or has adjourned for any period in excess of three calendar days, the Speaker of the House of Representatives and the President pro tempore of the Senate, if they deem it advisable (or if petitioned by at least 30 percent of the membership of their respective Houses) shall jointly request the President to convene Congress in order that it may consider the report and take appropriate action pursuant to this section.

(b) Within sixty calendar days after a report is submitted or is required to be submitted pursuant to section 4(a)(1), whichever is earlier, the President shall terminate any use of United States Armed Forces with respect to which such report was submitted (or required to be submitted), unless the Congress (1) has declared war or has enacted a specific authorization for such use of United States Armed Forces, (2) has extended by law such sixty-day period, or (3) is physically unable to meet as a result of an armed attack upon the United States. Such sixty-day period shall be extended for not more than an additional thirty days if the President determines and certifies to the Congress in writing that unavoidable military necessity respecting the safety of United States Armed Forces requires the continued use of such armed forces in the course of bringing about a prompt removal of such forces.

(c) Notwithstanding subsection (b), at any time that United States Armed Forces are engaged in hostilities outside the territory of the United States, its possessions and territories without a declaration of war or specific statutory authorization, such forces shall be removed by the President if the Congress so directs by concurrent resolution.

November 7, 1973   - 3 -   Pub. Law 93-148

CONGRESSIONAL PRIORITY PROCEDURES FOR JOINT RESOLUTION OR BILL

SEC. 6. (a) Any joint resolution or bill introduced pursuant to section 5(b) at least thirty calendar days before the expiration of the sixty-day period specified in such section shall be referred to the Committee on Foreign Affairs of the House of Representatives or the Committee on Foreign Relations of the Senate, as the case may be, and such committee shall report one such joint resolution or bill, together with its recommendations, not later than twenty-four calendar days before the expiration of the sixty-day period specified in such section, unless such House shall otherwise determine by the yeas and nays.

(b) Any joint resolution or bill so reported shall become the pending business of the House in question (in the case of the Senate the time for debate shall be equally divided between the proponents and the opponents), and shall be voted on within three calendar days thereafter, unless such House shall otherwise determine by yeas and nays.

(c) Such a joint resolution or bill passed by one House shall be referred to the committee of the other House named in subsection (a) and shall be reported out not later than fourteen calendar days before the expiration of the sixty-day period specified in section 5(b). The joint resolution or bill so reported shall become the pending business of the House in question and shall be voted on within three calendar days after it has been reported, unless such House shall otherwise determine by yeas and nays.

(d) In the case of any disagreement between the two Houses of Congress with respect to a joint resolution or bill passed by both Houses, conferees shall be promptly appointed and the committee of conference shall make and file a report with respect to such resolution or bill not later than four calendar days before the expiration of the sixty-day period specified in section 5(b). In the event the conferees are unable to agree within 48 hours, they shall report back to their respective Houses in disagreement. Notwithstanding any rule in either House concerning the printing of conference reports in the Record or concerning any delay in the consideration of such reports, such report shall be acted on by both Houses not later than the expiration of such sixty-day period.

CONGRESSIONAL PRIORITY PROCEDURES FOR CONCURRENT RESOLUTION

SEC. 7. (a) Any concurrent resolution introduced pursuant to section 5(c) shall be referred to the Committee on Foreign Affairs of the House of Representatives or the Committee on Foreign Relations of the Senate, as the case may be, and one such concurrent resolution shall be reported out by such committee together with its recommendations within fifteen calendar days, unless such House shall otherwise determine by the yeas and nays.

(b) Any concurrent resolution so reported shall become the pending business of the House in question (in the case of the Senate the time for debate shall be equally divided between the proponents and the opponents) and shall be voted on within three calendar days thereafter, unless such House shall otherwise determine by yeas and nays.

(c) Such a concurrent resolution passed by one House shall be referred to the committee of the other House named in subsection (a) and shall be reported out by such committee together with its recommendations within fifteen calendar days and shall thereupon become the pending business of such House and shall be voted upon within three calendar days, unless such House shall otherwise determine by yeas and nays.

(d) In the case of any disagreement between the two Houses of Congress with respect to a concurrent resolution passed by both Houses, conferees shall be promptly appointed and the committee of conference shall make and file a report with respect to such concurrent resolution within six calendar days after the legislation is referred to the committee of conference. Notwithstanding any rule in either House concerning the printing of conference reports in the Record or concerning any delay in the consideration of such reports, such report shall be acted on by both Houses not later than six calendar days after the conference report is filed. In the event the conferees are unable to agree within 48 hours, they shall report back to their respective Houses in disagreement.

INTERPRETATION OF JOINT RESOLUTION

SEC. 8. (a) Authority to introduce United States Armed Forces into hostilities or into situations wherein involvement in hostilities is clearly indicated by the circumstances shall not be inferred—

(1) from any provision of law (whether or not in effect before the date of the enactment of this joint resolution), including any provision contained in any appropriation Act, unless such provision specifically authorizes the introduction of United States Armed Forces into hostilities or into such situations and states that it is intended to constitute specific statutory authorization within the meaning of this joint resolution; or

(2) from any treaty heretofore or hereafter ratified unless such treaty is implemented by legislation specifically authorizing the introduction of United States Armed Forces into hostilities or into such situations and stating that it is intended to constitute specific statutory authorization within the meaning of this joint resolution.

(b) Nothing in this joint resolution shall be construed to require any further specific statutory authorization to permit members of United States Armed Forces to participate jointly with members of the armed forces of one or more foreign countries in the headquarters operations of high-level military commands which were established prior to the date of enactment of this joint resolution and pursuant to the United Nations Charter or any treaty ratified by the United States prior to such date.

(c) For purposes of this joint resolution, the term "introduction of United States Armed Forces" includes the assignment of members of such armed forces to command, coordinate, participate in the movement of, or accompany the regular or irregular military forces of any foreign country or government when such military forces are engaged, or there exists an imminent threat that such forces will become engaged, in hostilities.

(d) Nothing in this joint resolution—

(1) is intended to alter the constitutional authority of the Congress or of the President, or the provisions of existing treaties; or

(2) shall be construed as granting any authority to the President with respect to the introduction of United States Armed Forces into hostilities or into situations wherein involvement in hostilities is clearly indicated by the circumstances which authority he would not have had in the absence of this joint resolution.

SEPARABILITY CLAUSE

SEC. 9. If any provision of this joint resolution or the application thereof to any person or circumstance is held invalid, the remainder of the joint resolution and the application of such provision to any other person or circumstance shall not be affected thereby.

EFFECTIVE DATE

SEC. 10. This joint resolution shall take effect on the date of its enactment.

CARL ALBERT
Speaker of the House of Representatives.

JAMES O. EASTLAND
President of the Senate pro tempore.

IN THE HOUSE OF REPRESENTATIVES, U.S.,
November 7, 1973.

The House of Representatives having proceeded to reconsider the resolution (H. J. Res. 542) entitled "Joint resolution concerning the war powers of Congress and the President", returned by the President of the United States with his objections, to the House of Representatives, in which it originated, it was

Resolved, That the said resolution pass, two-thirds of the House of Representatives agreeing to pass the same.

Attest:

W. PAT JENNINGS
Clerk.

I certify that this Joint Resolution originated in the House of Representatives.

W. PAT JENNINGS
Clerk.

IN THE SENATE OF THE UNITED STATES
November 7, 1973.

The Senate having proceeded to reconsider the joint resolution (H. J. Res. 542) entitled "Joint resolution concerning the war powers of Congress and the President", returned by the President of the United States with his objections to the House of Representatives, in which it originated, it was

Resolved, That the said joint resolution pass, two-thirds of the Senators present having voted in the affirmative.

Attest:

                              FRANCIS R. VALEO
                                         Secretary.

LEGISLATIVE HISTORY:

HOUSE REPORTS: No. 93-287 (Comm. on Foreign Affairs) and No. 93-547 (Comm. of Conference).
SENATE REPORT No. 93-220 accompanying S. 440 (Comm. on Foreign Relations).
CONGRESSIONAL RECORD, Vol. 119 (1973):
    June 25, July 18, considered and passed House.
    July 18 - 20, considered and passed Senate, amended, in lieu of S. 440.
    Oct. 10, Senate agreed to conference report.
    Oct. 12, House agreed to conference report.
WEEKLY COMPILATION OF PRESIDENTIAL DOCUMENTS, Vol. 9, No. 43:
    Oct. 24, vetoed; Presidential message.
CONGRESSIONAL RECORD, Vol. 119 (1973):
    Nov. 7, House and Senate overrode veto.

KF
5060
.A25
1978

Holt, Pat M.
 The War powers
resolution

Cover and